ATLANTA FALCONS

ELLIOTT SMITH

WWW.APEXEDITIONS.COM

Copyright © 2025 by Apex Editions, Mendota Heights, MN 55120. All rights reserved. No part of this book may be reproduced or utilized in any form or by any means without written permission from the publisher.

Apex is distributed by North Star Editions:
sales@northstareditions.com | 888-417-0195

Produced for Apex by Red Line Editorial.

Photographs ©: Danny Karnik/AP Images, cover, 1; Paul Abell/AP Images, 4–5, 58–59; Kevin C. Cox/Getty Images Sport/Getty Images, 6–7, 32–33, 50–51, 54–55; Bob Verlin/Getty Images Sport/Getty Images, 8–9, 10–11; AP Images, 12–13; Gin Ellis/Getty Images Sport/Getty Images, 14–15; Al Bello/Getty Images Sport/Getty Images, 16–17; Bruce Bennett/Getty Images Studios/Getty Images, 18–19; Focus On Sport/Getty Images Sport/ Getty Images, 20–21, 24–25, 27; George Rose/Getty Images Sport/Getty Images, 22–23; Jonathan Daniel/Getty Images Sport/Getty Images, 28–29; Scott Halleran/Getty Images Sport/Getty Images, 30–31; Shutterstock Images, 34–35; Aaron M. Sprecher/AP Images, 37, 57; Joe Murphy/ NFLPhotoLibrary/Getty Images Sport/Getty Images, 38–39; Mike Ehrmann/ Getty Images Sport/Getty Images, 40–41; Doug Benc/Getty Images Sport/ Getty Images, 42–43; Cooper Neill/Getty Images Sport/Getty Images, 44–45; Rob Carr/Getty Images Sport/Getty Images, 47; Todd Kirkland/Getty Images Sport/Getty Images, 48–49, 52–53

Library of Congress Control Number: 2023921784

ISBN
979-8-89250-148-4 (hardcover)
979-8-89250-165-1 (paperback)
979-8-89250-289-4 (ebook pdf)
979-8-89250-182-8 (hosted ebook)

Printed in the United States of America
Mankato, MN
012025

NOTE TO PARENTS AND EDUCATORS

Apex books are designed to build literacy skills in striving readers. Exciting, high-interest content attracts and holds readers' attention. The text is carefully leveled to allow students to achieve success quickly.

TABLE OF CONTENTS

CHAPTER 1
RISE UP 4

CHAPTER 2
EARLY HISTORY 8

CHAPTER 3
LEGENDS 18

PLAYER SPOTLIGHT
DEION SANDERS 26

CHAPTER 4
RECENT HISTORY 28

PLAYER SPOTLIGHT
MATT RYAN 36

CHAPTER 5
MODERN STARS 38

PLAYER SPOTLIGHT
JULIO JONES 46

CHAPTER 6
TEAM TRIVIA 48

TEAM RECORDS • 56
TIMELINE • 58
COMPREHENSION QUESTIONS • 60
GLOSSARY • 62
TO LEARN MORE • 63
ABOUT THE AUTHOR • 63
INDEX • 64

CHAPTER 1
RISE UP

The fans rise to their feet. Nearly everyone is dressed in red and black. They cheer at the top of their lungs. "RISE UP" circles the stadium on huge screens. This is the official slogan of the Atlanta Falcons.

The Atlanta Falcons' slogan pumps fans up before kickoff.

Younghoe Koo (6) kicks the winning field goal during a 2023 game against the Green Bay Packers.

The game is nearly over. The Falcons are down two points. But kicker Younghoe Koo gets ready. The ball is snapped. Koo kicks. The field goal is good! Atlanta has come back to win the game. Falcons fans cheer loudly.

CHAPTER 2

EARLY HISTORY

The first NFL teams were mostly in the Northeast and Midwest. By the 1960s, the league wanted teams in the South. So, the NFL gave a team to Atlanta, Georgia. The Falcons began play in 1966.

Falcons players clash with the Baltimore Colts during a 1966 game.

The Falcons' early years were difficult. They won just 16 games in their first five seasons. Atlanta finally had a winning season in 1971. The team still finished in third place. But the Falcons were popular. They sold out most of their games.

LANDING ON THE FALCON

Atlanta held a naming contest for the new team. People from all over sent in ideas. Many suggested the Falcons. The winner was a teacher. She described falcons as brave and fierce.

Falcons running back Cannonball Butler (33) takes the handoff in a 1971 game against the New Orleans Saints.

Steve Bartkowski (10) threw two touchdown passes during the Falcons' first playoff game in 1978.

The Falcons had a breakthrough in 1978. They finished 9–7. That led them to the playoffs for the first time. The Falcons won their first-ever postseason game. They beat the Philadelphia Eagles. Then, in 1980, Atlanta won its first division title. But the Falcons lost in the playoffs. The Dallas Cowboys beat them 30–27.

The Falcons struggled for most of the 1980s. They bottomed out in 1989. That year, they went 3–13. But the team bounced back in 1991. Atlanta made the playoffs for the first time in nine years.

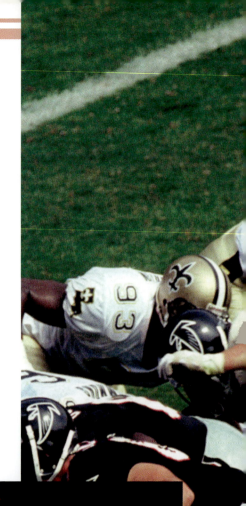

MAN IN BLACK

In 1990, Atlanta hired Jerry Glanville as head coach. He helped create a new team identity. The Falcons switched to black uniforms. They began focusing on defense, too. Glanville's ideas worked for a while. Atlanta made the playoffs in 1991. But Glanville was fired after the 1993 season.

The Falcons had used black jerseys before the 1990s. But in 1990, they switched to black helmets for the first time.

The 1998 Falcons lost just two games in the regular season. The conference championship game was close. Atlanta won in overtime. That victory took the Falcons to their first Super Bowl. But the dream season ended with a loss. Atlanta fell to the Denver Broncos.

THE DIRTY BIRDS

In 1998, running back Jamal Anderson had a great season. He celebrated touchdowns by flapping his arms. This dance became known as the Dirty Bird. Before long, "Dirty Birds" turned into a nickname for the entire team.

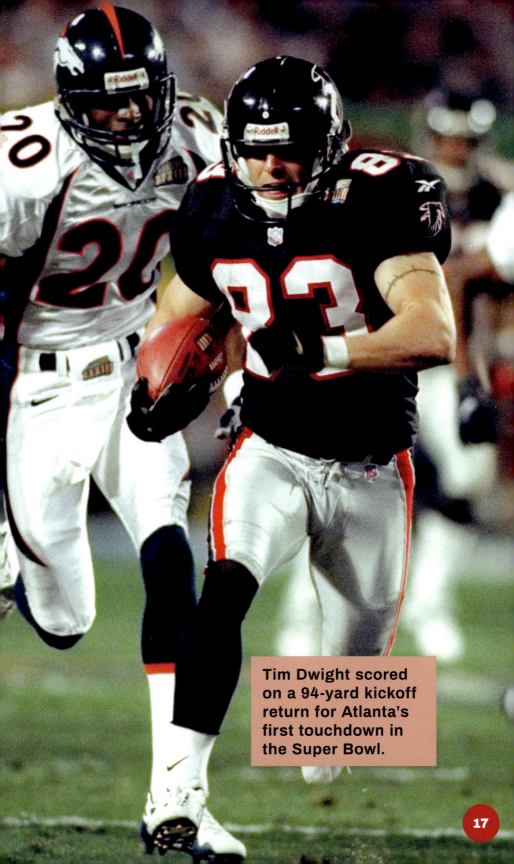

Tim Dwight scored on a 94-yard kickoff return for Atlanta's first touchdown in the Super Bowl.

CHAPTER 3
LEGENDS

Many talented players have suited up for the Falcons. In their first season, the Falcons had the No. 1 draft pick. They took linebacker Tommy Nobis. Nobis made 294 tackles in his first season. He also won the NFL's Rookie of the Year Award. Nobis became very popular in Atlanta. Fans called him "Mr. Falcon."

Tommy Nobis played all of his 11 seasons with Atlanta. The team retired his No. 60.

Claude Humphrey barrels toward the quarterback during a 1976 game.

Claude Humphrey was one of the best defenders in Falcons history. The defensive end made six Pro Bowls. He retired in 1981. Back then, sacks were not an official statistic. But records show Humphrey racked up 99.5 sacks with the Falcons. He entered the Pro Football Hall of Fame in 2014.

Steve Bartkowski passes during a 1983 game against the Rams.

The Falcons needed years to find a great quarterback. They finally got one in 1975. Steve Bartkowski was the No. 1 pick in the draft that year. And that was just the beginning. In 1980, he led the NFL with 31 touchdown passes. Bartkowski guided the Falcons to their first playoff appearances.

WHITE SHOES

Billy Johnson was a speedy wide receiver and punt returner. He loved wearing white cleats. He also danced after big plays. "White Shoes" Johnson brought fun to the struggling Falcons in the 1980s.

Running back Gerald Riggs joined the Falcons in 1982. He was known for his hard-charging style. Riggs spent seven seasons with the team. He was the key to Atlanta's ground game. In 1985, he ran for more than 1,000 yards. And he didn't fumble once. He was the only running back to do that in the 1980s.

THE HAMMER

Jessie Tuggle signed with the Falcons in 1987. The linebacker had not been drafted. But he dominated in his 14 seasons with Atlanta. He finished with more than 1,800 tackles.

In 1985, Gerald Riggs made the first of three straight Pro Bowls.

PLAYER SPOTLIGHT

DEION SANDERS

One of the NFL's flashiest players got his start with the Falcons. Deion Sanders became known as "Prime Time." The cornerback was Atlanta's top draft pick in 1989. He spent five seasons with the team. In that time, he intercepted 24 passes. Sanders also thrilled fans as a return man. In his first game, he returned a punt for a touchdown.

Sanders was a two-sport athlete. He also played in Major League Baseball. In 1992, he helped the Atlanta Braves reach the World Series.

DEION SANDERS ENTERED THE PRO FOOTBALL HALL OF FAME IN 2011.

CHAPTER 4

RECENT HISTORY

Atlanta mostly lost from 1999 to 2001. But the Falcons reached the playoffs again in the 2002 season. They faced the Green Bay Packers. The Packers had never lost a playoff game at home. But the Falcons changed that. Atlanta won the game easily.

Atlanta's defense held the Packers to one touchdown during the playoffs in January 2003.

Falcons players dump Gatorade on coach Mike Smith during their 13th regular-season victory of the 2010 season.

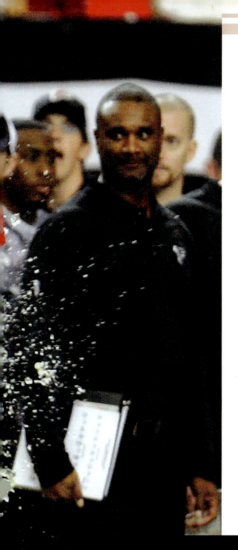

One of the greatest stretches in Falcons history happened from 2008 to 2012. The Falcons made the playoffs in four of those five seasons. In 2010 and 2012, they cruised to 13–3 records. But they couldn't get back to the Super Bowl.

SIDELINE STANDOUT

The Falcons hired Mike Smith as head coach in 2008. It was Smith's first head coaching job. He led Atlanta for seven seasons. He became the winningest coach in team history.

Atlanta's 2016 season was one to remember. It was also one to forget. The Falcons finished first in the division. Then they made it all the way to the Super Bowl.

The Falcons faced the New England Patriots. Atlanta held a 28–3 lead late in the third quarter. But the Patriots charged back. They won the game in overtime. It was a crushing loss for the Falcons and their fans.

Falcons running back Devonta Freeman soars into the end zone during the Super Bowl.

The Falcons' new stadium (right) was built next to the Georgia Dome.

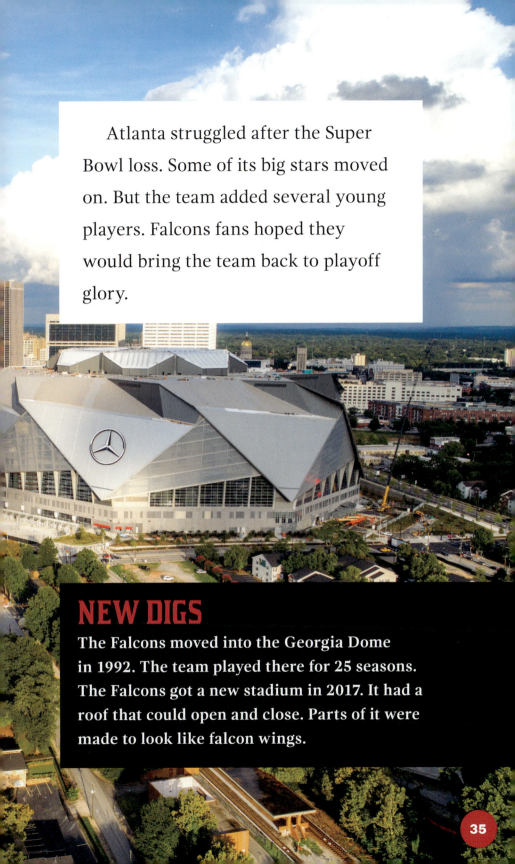

Atlanta struggled after the Super Bowl loss. Some of its big stars moved on. But the team added several young players. Falcons fans hoped they would bring the team back to playoff glory.

NEW DIGS

The Falcons moved into the Georgia Dome in 1992. The team played there for 25 seasons. The Falcons got a new stadium in 2017. It had a roof that could open and close. Parts of it were made to look like falcon wings.

PLAYER SPOTLIGHT

MATT RYAN

Matt Ryan was the greatest quarterback in Falcons history. He was the team's first draft pick in 2008. Right out of the gate, Ryan was a star. He won the Rookie of the Year Award.

Ryan spent 14 seasons with the team. He ended up owning all the Falcons' passing records. He threw for 59,735 yards with Atlanta. Ryan's best year came in 2016. He threw for nearly 5,000 yards that season. And he gave up just seven interceptions. He won the Most Valuable Player (MVP) Award. He became the first Falcons MVP in the team's 50-year history. Then Ryan led the Falcons to the Super Bowl.

MATT RYAN THREW 367 TOUCHDOWN PASSES DURING HIS FALCONS CAREER.

CHAPTER 5
MODERN STARS

Quarterback Michael Vick was Atlanta's top draft pick in 2001. His energy electrified Falcons fans. Vick became the first quarterback to rush for more than 1,000 yards in a season. He also led Atlanta to the 2004 conference championship game.

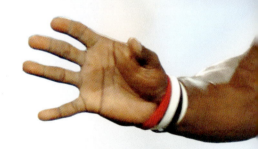

Michael Vick passes the ball during a 2004 game.

Tight end Tony Gonzalez joined the Falcons in 2009. Gonzalez brought veteran leadership to the team. He spent five seasons with Atlanta. He had at least 70 catches each year. He was also named to the All-Decade Team of the 2000s.

KICKIN' IT

Kicker Morten Andersen played in Atlanta for two different stretches. In 1998, his field goal sent Atlanta to the Super Bowl. Andersen scored 804 points as a Falcon.

Tony Gonzalez catches a touchdown pass in a January 2013 playoff game against Seattle.

Roddy White celebrates with a backflip after a touchdown in a January 2009 playoff game.

Wide receiver Roddy White was one of the NFL's most dependable players. He tallied at least 1,100 receiving yards for six straight seasons. White spent his entire 11-year career with Atlanta. He caught more than 800 passes during that time. He also set the team record for touchdowns with 63. White's talent went past the numbers. He was as clutch as they come. He made big plays when Atlanta needed him most.

Atlanta drafted offensive lineman Chris Lindstrom in 2019. He improved each season. In 2022, he became the league's top-ranked guard. In 2023, rookie running back Bijan Robinson gave fans plenty to cheer about. He piled up more than 1,400 total yards. In 2024, Atlanta signed quarterback Kirk Cousins. Falcons fans hoped he could lead the team to glory.

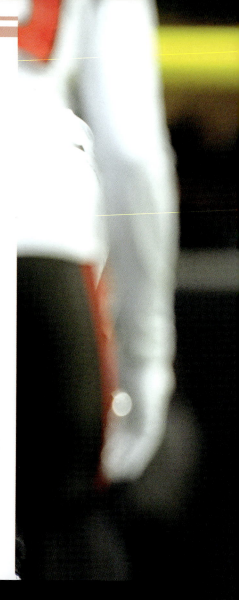

TOP KICKER

In 2019, Younghoe Koo became the latest in a line of great Falcons kickers. Koo was one of the league's most accurate kickers. In 2020 and 2021, he made more than 90 percent of his field goal attempts.

Chris Lindstrom made his first Pro Bowl in the 2022 season.

45

PLAYER SPOTLIGHT

JULIO JONES

Julio Jones was one of the most dangerous weapons in Falcons history. The wide receiver dazzled in all 10 of his seasons in Atlanta. At 6-foot-3 (191 cm), he was taller than many defenders. That let him nab catches over their heads. But Jones's height was just the start. He also had blazing speed. He ran excellent routes. And he had great hands.

In 2016, Jones had 300 receiving yards in one game. He became just the sixth player in NFL history to do that. Jones led the league in receiving yards in 2015 and 2018.

JULIO JONES RECORDED 10,000 CAREER YARDS FASTER THAN ANY OTHER RECEIVER IN NFL HISTORY.

CHAPTER 6
TEAM TRIVIA

The Falcons' biggest rivalry is with the New Orleans Saints. It is an exciting clash of teams from two major Southern cities. Entering 2024, the teams had played each other 110 times. They were tied 55–55.

The Falcons play the New Orleans Saints twice every season.

The Carolina Panthers are another NFC South opponent. Entering 2024, the Falcons were 36–22 against them.

The Falcons have changed divisions several times. Early on, their division didn't make much sense. The Falcons started out in the Coastal Division. The Baltimore Colts were the closest team to Atlanta. But the other two teams were in California.

In 1970, the Falcons moved to the NFC West. But Georgia touches the East Coast. Finally, in 2002, the Falcons moved to the NFC South.

The Falcons' first mascot was a live bird. But during a practice in 1966, the bird got scared. It flew away. The bird was found on top of a factory. Even so, the team continued to use a live falcon through the 1970s.

MASCOT MANIA

Atlanta's current mascot is Freddie Falcon. He has been the mascot for decades. He also visits schools, hospitals, and other places around Atlanta.

Freddie Falcon helps get Atlanta fans excited before a 2022 game.

Samuel L. Jackson performs "Rise Up" before a 2011 game against the Eagles.

One of the Falcons' biggest fans is actor Samuel L. Jackson. He often goes to games. Jackson also helped the team record several hype videos. He tells fans to "Rise Up."

FEELING HUNGRY?

Falcons fans can enjoy great deals at home games. The team has the NFL's cheapest food and drink prices. In 2023, hot dogs, pretzels, and sodas were all just $2 each.

TEAM RECORDS

All-Time Passing Yards: 59,735
  Matt Ryan (2008–21)

All-Time Touchdown Passes: 367
  Matt Ryan (2008–21)

All-Time Rushing Yards: 6,631
  Gerald Riggs (1982–88)

All-Time Receiving Yards: 12,896
  Julio Jones (2011–20)

All-Time Receptions: 848
  Julio Jones (2011–20)

All-Time Receiving Touchdowns: 63
  Roddy White (2005–15)

All-Time Interceptions: 39
  Rolland Lawrence (1973–80)

All-Time Sacks: 99.5*
  Claude Humphrey (1968–78)

All-Time Scoring: 1,163
  Matt Bryant (2009–19)

All-Time Coaching Wins: 66
  Mike Smith (2008–14)

Sacks were not an official statistic until 1982. However, researchers have studied old games to determine sacks dating back to 1960.

All statistics are accurate through 2023.

TIMELINE

1966   **1971**   **1978**   **1980**   **1989**

The Falcons play their first NFL game. They lose to the Los Angeles Rams 19–14.

The Falcons reach the playoffs for the first time.

Deion Sanders becomes a Falcon as the team's top draft pick.

The Falcons record the first winning season in team history, with a 7–6–1 record.

The Falcons win their first division title with a 12–4 record.

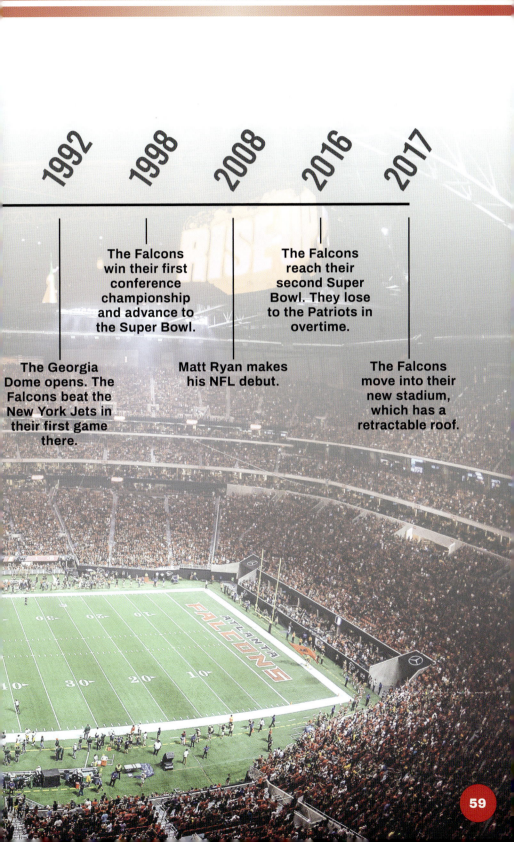

1992 — The Georgia Dome opens. The Falcons beat the New York Jets in their first game there.

1998 — The Falcons win their first conference championship and advance to the Super Bowl.

2008 — Matt Ryan makes his NFL debut.

2016 — The Falcons reach their second Super Bowl. They lose to the Patriots in overtime.

2017 — The Falcons move into their new stadium, which has a retractable roof.

59

COMPREHENSION QUESTIONS

Write your answers on a separate piece of paper.

1. Write a paragraph that explains the main ideas of Chapter 4.

2. What do you think is the most important moment in Atlanta Falcons history? Why?

3. Which player was the Falcons' first-ever draft pick?

   A. Deion Sanders
   B. Tommy Nobis
   C. Matt Ryan

4. Why is good route running important for a wide receiver?

   A. It helps them make tackles.
   B. It helps them come up with new plays.
   C. It helps them get away from defenders.

5. What does **clutch** mean in this book?

*He was as **clutch** as they come. He made big plays when Atlanta needed him most.*

    A. playing against a bad team

    B. scaring another player

    C. succeeding in a tough time

6. What does **accurate** mean in this book?

*Koo was one of the league's most **accurate** kickers. In 2020 and 2021, he made more than 90 percent of his field goal attempts.*

    A. mistake-free

    B. powerful

    C. fast

Answer key on page 64.

GLOSSARY

conference
A group of teams that make up part of a sports league.

division
In the NFL, a group of teams that make up part of a conference.

intercepted
Caught an opponent's pass as a defensive player.

league
A group of teams that play one another and compete for a championship.

overtime
An extra period that happens if two teams are tied at the end of the fourth quarter.

rivalry
An ongoing competition that brings out strong emotion from fans and players.

routes
Paths that receivers take so they can get open and catch the ball.

sacks
Plays that happen when a defender tackles the quarterback before he can throw the ball.

slogan
A phrase used by a group to attract attention.

veteran
A person who has been doing his or her job for a long time and has a lot of experience.

TO LEARN MORE

BOOKS

Adamson, Thomas. *The Atlanta Falcons.* Minneapolis: Bellwether Media, 2024.

Olson, Ethan. *Great NFL Super Bowl Championships.* San Diego: BrightPoint Press, 2024.

Streeter, Anthony. *Super Bowl All-Time Greats.* Mendota Heights, MN: Press Box Books, 2025.

ONLINE RESOURCES

Visit **www.apexeditions.com** to find links and resources related to this title.

ABOUT THE AUTHOR

Elliott Smith is a writer who lives just outside Washington, DC, with his wife and two children. He used to be a sports reporter, and he covered athletes from high school to the pros. He loves reading, watching sports on TV and in person, going to concerts, and collecting sports jerseys.

INDEX

Andersen, Morten, 40
Anderson, Jamal, 16

Bartkowski, Steve, 23

Cousins, Kirk, 44

Dallas Cowboys, 13
Denver Broncos, 16

Freddie Falcon, 52

Georgia Dome, 35
Glanville, Jerry, 14
Gonzalez, Tony, 40
Green Bay Packers, 29

Humphrey, Claude, 21

Jackson, Samuel L., 55
Johnson, Billy, 23
Jones, Julio, 46

Koo, Younghoe, 7, 44

Lindstrom, Chris, 44

New England Patriots, 32
New Orleans Saints, 49
Nobis, Tommy, 18

Philadelphia Eagles, 13

Riggs, Gerald, 24
Robinson, Bijan, 44
Ryan, Matt, 36

Sanders, Deion, 26
Smith, Mike, 31
Super Bowl, 16, 31–32, 35, 36, 40

Tuggle, Jessie, 24

Vick, Michael, 38

White, Roddy, 43

ANSWER KEY:

1. Answers will vary; 2. Answers will vary; 3. B; 4. C; 5. C; 6. A